Thank you
for a
wonderful
year!

Made in the USA
Middletown, DE
05 May 2022

65304836R00064